EVERYONE NEEDS A PET

EVERYONE NEEDS A PET

Jane Coffey

PALMETTO
PUBLISHING
Charleston, SC
www.PalmettoPublishing.com

Copyright © 2024 by Jane Coffey

All rights reserved

No portion of this book may be reproduced, stored in a retrieval system, or transmitted in any form by any means—electronic, mechanical, photocopy, recording, or other—except for brief quotations in printed reviews, without prior permission of the author.

Paperback ISBN: 979-8-8229-4155-7

Thanks to:
Taryn Bintz for the cover
Bert Longbotham for his typing
I could not have done it without his help

MY STORY

I don't know who my parents were or where I was born (so you see, I'm not a pedigreed cat). My first recollection (I use big words because I went to college – but more of that later) was being in a big cage with many other cats at a place called the Schenectady Animal Shelter (I don't know what we were being sheltered from – human beings or other animals perhaps?)

Well, one day (it was Christmas Eve afternoon 1969) three young people – two good looking auburn haired girls and a nice looking young man –came through the Animal Shelter and stopped by my cage and looked at all of us cats. Then Barb, the older girl, pointed at me and said, "That's the one – look, she's a calico cat and I can see that she has great potential." I must admit that at that time I wasn't much to look at. I was scrawny and had a long tail that Barb's father said looked like a rat tail! Imagine such an insult!

The three young people put me in a box, paid five dollars as a contribution to the Animal Shelter, and took me home. I didn't care too much for that car ride, but felt that I was looking forward to a promising future.

When they brought me into the house, Their father said, "No, not another cat in this house!" (They already had a cat and a dog!) I could see that I was going to have to win him over – and I did – he later became my favorite person!

Barb said, "Oh, that's all right, Dad. She's not going to live here; I'm taking her to college with me." So, supposedly, my future was all settled for the next few years!

The next few days were fun. There was a Christmas tree with shiny red balls to paw and Christmas morning there was so much paper to jump into! It rattled so nicely! What's more, Barb's Mom made me a catnip mouse as she did every year after that. Do you know what fun it is to rip that felt all apart so that catnip comes out on the floor and you can roll in it? It's ecstasy! Of course, Barb's Dad always disapproved of the catnip on the floor! Didn't I tell you I had to work hard to win him over?

Say, I must tell you about my name. First Barb was going to call me "Pookey", but her Mom thought that sounded too much like Pukey (I guess that name would have been appropriate later on), so the whole family agreed that Samantha

(Sam for short) would be better. Several years later Barb's Mom (who later became my Mistress) added "Jane" as my middle name. That was like my two Mistresses – Barbara Jane and Florence Jane. Sometimes Kittie, Barb's sister, and Mistress of the Other Cat, Shenanigans, called me "Sambucca". I'd answer to any name (when I felt like it!)

I should also describe what I look like. I turned out to be a very beautiful cat – at least, that's what people always said – I'm not being vain. I'm a calico cat – that means three colors: yellow, white and black. I have white paws, a black tail, a pretty white face with yellow ears and black and yellow spots on top of my head and white whiskers. Mistress Jane always said I was very photogenic (that means I photograph well) and took lots of pictures of me. She even made miniature figures of me to put in miniature room box scenes for Barb and Master Bill, but goodness, I'm getting way ahead of myself – that's far in the future.

You remember that Barb told her Dad that she was going to take me to college? And she did! What an experience!

Barb was a junior at the University of Rochester in Rochester, New York. After Christmas vacation, she went back to school by bus. Of course, I went along! She carried me on the bus in a cloth tote bag so the driver wouldn't see me. She also had a shoe box of kitty litter, as she knew I might have to "go" on the four hour trip. And you guessed it, I did have to use the kitty litter! The passengers around Barb began to look around uneasily – wondering where that smell was coming from!

I lived in the college dormitory that semester, through the summer term and part of the next fall term. That summer Barb had a car – a 1961 Lancer – so our trips back and forth were a little easier. We lived on the ninth floor and I loved looking out the window at the scenery far down below. Too bad I wasn't watching and could warn my Mistress the night someone stole the battery out of her car.

Barb used to bring me scraps from her meals in the dining room to supplement my dry cat food diet. So you know what, I even ate lettuce!

That fall we moved into a suite (that's several rooms with living room, bathroom, bedrooms and a kitchenette) in another dormitory. What fun I had there! I would run the whole length of the hall, across the living room and straight up to the top of the drapes! Another game I played (which gave me good practice for a later activity) was to take the girl's socks or underwear in my mouth and drag them around to other places in the suite! Well, that did it! The other girls complained so much when they couldn't find their clothes that I was expelled from the University of Rochester and came to Ballston Lake! So – I had a new Mistress and Master now!

I also had to share my new home with another cat and a dog! Shenanegans was a cat owned by Barb's sister, Kittie, and Max was the dog belonging to her brother, Dick. You see, each child in the family had an animal and then they went away to college and left the animals home with Mom, Jane and Dad, Bill. Max wasn't there all the time though as sometimes he lived in Ithaca with Dick.

Shenanigans and I got along pretty well – we mostly ignored each other – except at meal times. They would feed us both at the same time – mostly dry cat food – but I'd be so afraid Shenanigans would take some of mine that I'd bolt my food (that means easting it fast) so fast that it would disturb my stomach and I'd throw it up again! Poor Master or Mistress would have to clean up after me!

Max and I were good friends. I used to love to lie in-between his legs and cuddle up to him when he was lying on his rug in the dining room (that rug later on became my rug.) I must tell you how Max saved me one day – that's an interesting story!

One day (it was a Saturday afternoon if I remember correctly) Max and I were playing outside. A great big neighbor dog came and chased me and bit my tail! Oh, did it hurt! Max was called in the house, but I was so scared and hurt that I crouched down beside the garage and couldn't move! When Max, my friend got in the house, he told the family that I was hurt! Yes, he whined and whined and then brought Kittie and Mistress Jane out to show them where I was! They took me to the Vet's (I was so upset I wet all over Kittie's lap on the way), and I had to stay in the hospital overnight to have my tail fixed up. They gave me some kind of drug while I was being operated on so when I got home the next day I staggered around like I was drunk! Oh, well, it soon wore off! Thank goodness for Max who saved my life by chasing that big nasty dog off and reporting to my family!

I had favorite places to sit in our house. There was one right beside Master in his big yellow chair (I told you I'd win him over!) or on his lap while he watched the TV news. (He'd put a white blanket on his lap so I wouldn't get my white hairs all over his pants). I'd lay my head on his arm and look up at him lovingly – how to win friends and influence people!

Then there was the snug sack – that was another place. Mistress would fold it up and put it in the corner of the davenport (I guess that's the old fashioned name for it – some people nowadays call it a couch). I'd curl up on it and go to sleep – such soft comfort! Of course, sitting on Mistress's lap when she was reading the newspaper and had the snug sack around her was a daily morning routine!

Most of the time I was a pretty well-behaved cat, but I did have a few bad habits! One of the worst was sharpening my claws on the furniture! They did get me a scratching post, but I only liked the base of that and could dig it well! However, the yellow chair, hassock and edge of the couch just seemed so much more satisfactory! Master and Mistress will have some scratch marks to remember me by!

The other habit I had (which started in college) was carrying things. Master and Mistress used to sleep upstairs in the back bedroom and Master had a four drawer dresser in which he kept socks in the top drawer. He often left the drawer open an inch or so. I could jump up on Mistress's dresser, then to the taller dresser, put my paw in the drawer, pull out a pair of rolled up socks and carry them down the stairs to deposit them in the living room. I always announced this nice gift with a "Prrrt", so they'd know I was doing it for them. If Mistress didn't put the clean laundry away, I'd have many socks to bring downstairs. Dick used to say he was embarrassed to bring his friends home 'cause he didn't know what he might find spread around the living room floor! One time while Master and Mistress were having recorder practice here, I even brought one of Mistress's slips downstairs, dragging it between my legs, and announcing what I brought as I put it on my favorite rug in the dining room. I guess Mistress was embarrassed, but I thought it was great fun!

As you can see, I've had many interesting adventures. I can remember one camping trip the whole family went on. Master and Mistress had a trailer so we could all sleep together – except we cats usually slept in the station wagon. As I remember, we must have taken two cars and we "girls" (including us two cats) rode home in one car. Shenanigans and I didn't like all that movement and kept running around until Mistress Jane, who was driving, got really angry and said, "Get that cat out of here!"

The best trips of all, though were in Arvie, the big motor home. I really got so I enjoyed those trips and became an awfully good traveler, but my first experience wasn't the greatest!

It was in the fall of 1980, and Master and Mistress had just retired that summer. They planned a trip to Nova Scotia. Max was already gone to Doggie Heaven and Kittie consented to take Shenanigans (which made them decide to keep her), so nothing to do but take me along!

We started out on a warm day in early September and I certainly didn't like it much! Whoever heard off your house moving under you all the time! I cried and cried and cried and was really pretty scared! One time I tried to get up on Master's lap – he had shorts on so my claws dug into his leg! The air was pretty thick with heavy language there for a while! I had to cover my ears!

Mistress tried to hold me to comfort me and I finally decided I might as well accept the inevitable and stop crying! Besides, I was getting hoarse after two days of it!

When we got to our first campsite, Master thought I ought to go out for some fresh air, but I shivered and shook so much he had to hold me on his lap by the campfire and couldn't go bike riding with Mistress!

The second night we were in Houlton, Maine, and they decided I could be out on a leash and string! It was long enough so that I could get up on the wheel under Arvie! I got all greasy and Master was disgusted as he cleaned me up!

Then there was that time at Acadia National Park when Mistress tried to walk me on a leash! (She didn't understand that leashes are for dogs not cats; we're too independent!) I'd walk on the leash as long as she'd follow me back to the door of the RV!

Well, I got used to traveling in Arvie. We took trips every summer for six years. Mistress gave me a nice pink baby blanket at the foot of their upstairs bunk, and I'd sleep there while we were riding. I'd never fail to come down beside Master at meal time and sit right beside him up at the table! They even gave me my own plate with my name on it!

As I said, I got used to traveling. I even got so I liked to get out of Arvie and walk around! I remember one time in Canada I walked out the door, across the grassy campsite and into the tall grass across the road before Mistress caught up with me! Whenever the back door was open with the screen door closed, I'd sit by the hour watching the birds, the chipmunks and squirrels or people in other campsites.

There was that time at Pinery Provincial Park when Mistress's brother and wife, Ted and Ro, and daughter, Susan, were with us. Those chipmunks were so friendly they'd eat out of people's hands, but I couldn't stand the tension! I pushed the door open myself and gave chase!

That was the time also when Susan was sleeping on the bed made up from the table and I jumped down on her face in the middle of the night! I should have apologized for that as I know the Townsends weren't too crazy about cats, though Susan liked them better than the others did.

As you see I've had many experiences traveling and have been many thousands of miles. I think my Master figures I've probably traveled 25,000 miles at least in Arvie! Would you like to know some of the places I've been?

We've made several trips to Michigan as that's where Ted and Ro stay when they come back from India. One year we went to Flint, Michigan by car because it was too snowy to take Arvie. We stayed at Ro's mother's house and none of those people liked me too much, so I was cooped up in a little bedroom the whole week. I stayed under the bed most of the time. On the way out to Michigan we stayed in a motel and that was different.

In 1982 we went to the World's Fair in Knoxville, Tennessee and then down to Gulf Shores, Alabama and New Orleans! Those millions of love-bugs at Gulf Shores were something I'd never seen before – don't care if I don't ever see them again either! It was pretty hot too!

In the spring of 1983 we took a nice long western trip. We went to visit Master's cousin in Oklahoma and then on to the Grand Canyon and several other National Parks. See, I told you I was a well-traveled cat!

There were a couple of trips my Master and Mistress took that I couldn't go with them. After all, you can't take a cat on an airplane and a touring bus! When they went to England, I went to stay at Kittie's house. She had a husband and two little girls by this time and John really loved me – so did Bri and Taryn, but little girls are sometimes hard on old cats!

One time, Master and Mistress went to Germany, so a very nice girl from down the street, Alicia, and her boyfriend, Andy, came twice each day and fed and comforted me. I did miss Master and Mistress though!

I forgot to mention that years ago (that's why I forgot – it was so long ago), when both Shenanigans and I lived here, we'd just stay outside and in the garage when the family went away. A neighbor would come over to feed us. After all, we had each other, and do you know where we slept? – Under the hood of the old car!

Being such a well-educated cat, I used to also write letters (that was good practice for writing this story). I got a letter one day from Taffy, who belongs to one of Master and Mistress's recorder playing friends., Of course, I had to answer it and we corresponded back and forth several times.

Well, I guess I'm coming to the end of my story. I'm sixteen years old and have lived a good, full, adventurous life. I have kidney failure and am getting weaker every day, so I now know that Kittie Heaven isn't far away. But one can't expect much more when you have attained the equivalent of 112 years in human living. I've been an adorable, affectionate, active, adventurous (and that's only the "a's" –I bet I could go through the alphabet with more descriptive adjectives) pet and am ready now to cross the Rainbow Bridge and go to Animal Heaven to meet my friends, Max and Shenanigans and others like them. I know Master and Mistress and all their family will miss me very much, but they must remember the good things about our life together and how well they treated me and not regret my passing on.

PIPPIN, THE MIDDLE CAT

My name is Pippin Coffey and I now live in Kitty Heaven. I crossed the Rainbow Bridge 29 years ago. But, I had a wonderful life in those 7 years I lived with my beloved Master and Mistress, Bill and Jane Coffey. I am a very well educated cat like the other important cats in the Coffey's lives and that is why I can look down from Kitty Heaven to write my story. You see, my predecessor (pretty big word, right?), Samantha, (or Sam)

and the cat who shortly followed me (only 4 days later) have written their stories before they joined me here in Kitty Heaven.

The saying goes that the middle child doesn't always get as much attention as the First Born and the Youngest and now that shows that it applies to cats also! Hmph! That isn't quite fair, is it?

Now I arrived at the Coffey household in an unusual way! I arrived by airplane! No, the airplane didn't come to Charlton! The Coffey's oldest daughter came by airplane to the Albany Airport and when Barbara got off the plane she was carrying me in a cat carrier. I was a birthday present for her Mom. We stopped at MacDonald's for lunch and I got a good look at what a restaurant looked like there.

When I got to my new home, I had to take some time to investigate. I do like to use big words don't I? What a lot of fun to run back and forth down the hall and up and down the stairs. Boy, I thought, this is going to be a great place to live.

Now, you know what? We didn't always stay in that big house! We did a lot of traveling. We traveled in a big car called a Motorhome.

When we would start out, I would protest loudly for a while. But Mistress gave me a nice soft pink blanket (I'm glad it was pink as that is the color for females!). She put the pink blanket on the seat by the table so I could look out the window and see the sights as we traveled. Of course, I could take a nap there too, but sometimes I would sit on Mistress's lap in the front seat. I tried to sit on

Master's lap a couple of times but that was a "No, No." I might interfere with his driving.

Before I traveled, I had to go to a Veterinarian to get a rabies shot and when we traveled we had to take the papers with us to prove it. Ouch, that hurt and I let the Doctor know it!

One of my first trips was to Massachusetts to pick up Mistress's brother, Ted, and his wife, Rosemary. We did some traveling around near Boston before we got to Ted and Ro's daughter, Susan's house. Master and Mistress liked to have coffee in the morning so we found a place along the seashore by an interesting statue, "The Fisherman's Memorial –The Old Salt." I remember Mistress reading what it said on it – "They that go down to the sea in ships." That must be fun! Too bad I never got to do that!

Anyway, about the coffee drinking. Master must have been nervous or something as he spilled his whole cup of coffee all over himself and the table and seat cushion. Mistress Jane was kinda disgusted!!

One of the nice things that happened while we were in Massachusetts (my, that's a big word to spell) was the family that was there celebrated Mistress Jane's 68th birthday. (She is 99 now so, you see, that was a long time ago.) Of course, I didn't go – just stayed in the Honey Motorhome, but I heard all about it. Mistress writes in a "logbook" every night and even writes down what they had to eat on special occasions. They went to The Wayside Inn, a nice, famous old Inn in Sudbury (where Susan and her family live) and had a great time.

The next morning Susan went out on a "bagel run" and we left to go back to NY after that! (I wouldn't have minded a taste of one of those bagels!)

On our way back to NY, Ted sat in the front seat with Master driving, of course, and Ro and Mistress sat at the table.

The next trip was to Pittsford, NY to visit Mistress Jane's cousins, John and Marion Brown. Of course, I just stayed in the RV while they traveled around in John's car to see the city. From there we went north and camped along the St. Lawrence River. I always looked out the window to see any interesting wildlife. Sometimes there were seagulls or geese. That's pretty exciting.

We stayed at one campsite where there was a tree full of birds to watch. Oh, yes, that was the campsite where I had a big adventure. When Mistress went out the door, she accidentally left it open and I decided to go out and explore! Neither Master or Mistress could find my hiding place and were very upset. Master even went to get a Ranger to help. Then a man in a campsite behind us called "Are you looking for your cat? She came on our site a while ago and is now in those bushes." He came into the bushes which were all thorny and prickly and Master rattled my dry food box and Mistress got me out of the bushes (with lots of scratches from the bushes.) They were so glad to find me.

On this trip we also went to Canada to visit an old fashioned village. On the way back coming to the St. Lawrence Locks, there was a station wagon (see, I know about cars also) in front of us with 3 young girls sitting in the back facing the back. They started waving, so Mistress brought me up to the windshield and they got all excited seeing me!

When I first joined Master Bill and Mistress Jane for travel we had the biggest of the three RV's they owned. It clocked up 71,000 miles (Master said that meant 3 times around the world. So he thought we should get a new and smaller one. So they bought one called a Honey.

Now, this one had a very different set up. It didn't have any upper bunk where all three of us used to sleep, but a couch that pulled out to make a double bed. Well, to tell the truth, it was narrower than a double bed and slightly dangerous as it just had one metal rod that held up the side that pulled out! (Oh my, that was a complicated explanation wasn't it?) It also had a big refrigerator (where my good wet food was kept) and, just imagine, a little bathroom with wash bowl, toilet and shower (of course, I didn't need the shower as I always kept myself very clean with my tongue!!)

We had a couple of "disasters" with that shower! If you weren't plugged into a drain, it would overflow and run out the back door. Master found that out soon enough. Then there was the time Mistress got locked in the bathroom while we were driving along a highway. She kept pounding on the door and Master thought there was something wrong with the tires and stopped – and let her out.

She usually came back mid-morning and boiled water in the teapot for morning coffee which they would drink while Mater was driving.

Now I found that I could have some fun with that bed, especially at night! I would crawl down between the two parts of the bed and then crawl on under the sink and stove. Wasn't that clever? Unfortunately, my folks didn't think so. I usually slept on my table seat pink blanket or on Master and Mistress's feet on their sleeping bag. How cozy and warm that was!

I think I was known as the cat who took the longest trip. Yes, I know, Cali (the third cat and the longest lived, went to Florida twice to visit Ted and Ro at Penny Retirement Center) but I am talking about a long trip at one time. I went to Cal-i-for-nia (what a long name for a state) and we had a lot of adventures!

One thing I liked a lot on all the camping trips was we would have evening campfires and all three of us would sit out by the campfire. Sometimes we would have tea and crackers or even popcorn. I, of course, would beg for a snack.

One time in Canada (yes, we traveled up there also) they went to a K-Mart store and bought me a red leash with straps that went across my back and under my belly! The first time I wore it outside I didn't like it and dragged my belly on the ground. Then I realized that the leash meant that I was going outside and since that was fun, I responded eagerly!!

One time we were visiting some cousins of Master's in Oklahoma and it was very hot! I got sick twice (throw up and diarrhea.) Poor Mistress and Master had to clean up my mess.. I had been allowed to stay in Cousin Liz's air conditioned Laundry Room while we were in Minco, Oklahoma which helped keep me from panting in the heat.

We headed on west and saw a Veterinary Clinic in Cordell, Oklahoma (I like to keep track of the route!) The Vet and his pretty blonde wife examined me and said it wasn't hairballs (something cats often get) or food poisoning so gave me some liquid medicine (Ugh!!!Pttph!!) and Master had to give me some more at night. I protested heartily at that awful tasting stuff but it did make me better.

We saw some interesting sights coming thru Arizona and into California. When I'm not napping I like to look out my window and see the palm trees and even some 1,000 year old lava beds! You see, Mistress likes to read from Guide Books and I remember these things!!

We took a special road for 86 miles from Seligman to Kingsman, Arizona. This was the old highway 66 which was the old main highway across the west. We even saw and felt a "devil dog" on that road. That is a mini sand tornado that really swayed Arvie! No wonder they're called "Devil Dogs" (Dogs can be devils sometimes.)

When we came in to Arizona (and also California) a man got under Arvie to check for gypsy moths. I should have offered to help him, but I guess he didn't find any!

Our first campsite in California was high up on a hill where you could see the Pacific Ocean. I liked that place as there were many black capped gulls that I got very excited about.

I like to sleep at night between Master and Mistress's pillows. It's nice and cozy! But, sometimes, I wake up and it's so boring I decide to run up and down on top of them. It's fun but they don't appreciate my fun! I also like to attack Mistress's pen when she is writing in her log. She should be playing with me instead of playing with a pen!

When we were still in New England (that's sorta up north from our home) we camped at a nice campground by a lake in Pawtuckaway (did that mean cat's paws??) in New Hampshire. When we got there the sign said "No Pets" (that's not nice for campgrounds!!) Master told a little black lie, as I'm mostly black fur. Anyway, when the Ranger (that's the man in charge of the campsite) came to find out if we were going to stay another day, Mistress thought she had better hide this "No Pet" so I was quickly put in the bathroom with my bowl and toys, so the Ranger would not know that I was there!

One of the "toys" Master made for me was a button on a string hung from the handle of a low door. I could bat it back and forth!! What fun!! Master and Mistress were not happy about that game if I played it at night!

Do you know that I had a ride on a boat? Of course, I was in my cat carrying case and went on a ferry from New Bedford, Massachusetts (there's that big state name again) to Cuttyhunk Island where we visited Master and Mistress's friends, the Lovells. I was very quiet on the ferry boat! The Lovells lived in a cottage high up on a hill with a great view of the harbor. Their cottage had 8 bedrooms, so we three Coffeys stayed in the last bedroom down the hall as the

Lovells had two cats and didn't want me to bother them. Too bad we couldn't play together but one was quite old and wouldn't have liked my rough and tumble playing!!

Master and Mistress decided to go to Seawall Campground in Acadia National Park after we left Lovell's hillside cottage. It rained a lot on the way and I could tell that traffic was very heavy. Master didn't like that kind of driving!

I guess that Master and Mistress had camped at Seawall before and really liked it. Well, I'll tell you about my adventure there and what fun I had!

One day Mistress had the picnic table outside all set up for lunch and I was running around wildly inside. Mistress left the door open when she went outside and I thought "Aha, here's my chance for exploring! I ran out the door, across the road behind and under an RV and car with everyone chasing after me. What fun!! Master caught me and put me in our RV but I did a lot of squeaking (that's the kind of Meow I make) because I didn't want to be inside when everyone was outside!

So, just to pay them back, I decided to carry and hide somethings (like my predecessor -big word) and they thought it was cute with her!! I took that red net dish scraper and one of Master's blue socks and hid them and brought them out a few days later!! Served them right.

From Seawall –Acadia we went on to Canada. One place we stayed was high on a hill at a place called Fire Islands. When Mistress gave me my supper I tried to go outside and Mistress grabbed me around the middle to stop me and

I then vomited all my supper right there in the doorway. It hurt my tummy and I couldn't help it. Sorry Mistress!

Oh yes, I remember another time that I had fun "getting into mischief" in that biggest RV (I know I'm jumping around a little in my story but these memories just come back to me that way.)

We were traveling with Ted and Ro (Mistress's brother and wife – they are both in Heaven now, much to Mistress's great sorrow and Master has been in Heaven seven years and Mistress sure misses him!) Anyway, back to my mischief story. In that big RV Ted and Ro slept on the pull-out back bed and Master and Mistress slept in the bed up over the front – it even had a curtain that could be drawn for privacy! Well, I got tired of sleeping so I decided to play with one of the toys (well, it really wasn't supposed to be a toy but I made it so.) After climbing all over everybody (Ted and Ro don't like cats so that didn't endear me to them) I started batting the fly swatter (which was hung on the low closet door) back and forth!! Mistress declared then and there, that my middle name was "Nuisance".

So I guess it's about time to end my story. I've gotten together with Samantha and Cali up here in Heaven and we all agree that we had wonderful lives with Mistress Jane and Master Bill Coffey. Thank you Master and Mistress for giving all of us cats such loving and caring homes!! No cat could ask for anything better.

Pippin Coffey's Story (with a little help from Mistress Jane Coffey)

THE ONE WHO RULED THE HOUSE

My name is Cali Coffey and I am now in Kitty Heaven. I crossed the Rainbow Bridge on Christmas Eve 2015. But I lived a long and adventurous life (I'm a well-educated cat though I didn't go to college like one of my predecessors, but I like to use big words) I hope the reader won't mind that!

Let me tell you how I came to this wonderful life. I don't know who my parents were or where I was born but I do remember being in a cage with some other cats. This nice looking couple came in and were looking at the cages with kittens in them. I thought, "Ah ha! This looks like a good possibility." (See how I like to use big words). I put my little paw out of the cage, meowed and thought, "Take me, take me." The lady said to the man, "This is the one. She's a calico (that means I

have three colors of fur and am a lady) isn't she cute?" The man agreed so the lady in the Animal Shelter (that's where this was) gave me a bath!! Brrr! Cats usually bathe themselves with their tongues and do that so much they are most always very clean.

Well, they wrapped me in a towel and the lady cuddled me on her lap as we rode in the car to my forever home.

Now this couple were Bill and Jane Coffey and they lived in a nice big house about two miles south of the Village of Charlton. It looked like a nice place to run down the halls and up and down the stairs and investigate things.

So I settled in to my great life. They put out a scratching post that their former cat, Pippin, (see story number two) had used. I didn't understand it so I thought it was more fun to climb up and sit on top of it. Scratching the sofa was more fun for my little claws but my owners did not like that!!

I guess I should tell you about my family – they were Master Bill Coffey and Mistress Jane Coffey. Master was a GE Engineer and worked at the GE Research Lab and Mistress taught music at Charlton Heights Elementary School not very far away from our house.

Master and Mistress had three children, Barbara, Kittie and Richard. They are all grown up and not living in Charlton anymore but, still love animals. At one time we had three pets at once – the girls had cats and the boy had a dog. They all got along fine together.

Barbara now always has two Siamese cats, male and female. Kittie had a cat until last year and one of her daughters has two cats - one a Bengal. The two of Kittie's other daughters have dogs. So you see, our family really loves pets. I'm very glad about that!

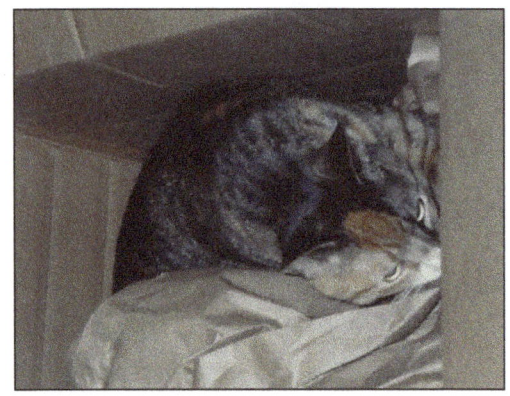

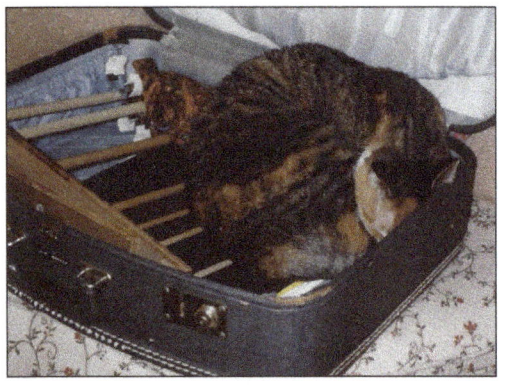

I want to tell you what I look like. Of course, Mistress counted all the pictures she has of me and would you believe it? There are 57 altogether. And do you know why I have so many more pictures in this book than my two predecessors (another big word you see!)? It's because I lived so much longer than they did! Don't you think that is right? You have already seen some at the first part of this book and there are many more to come! Poor Pippin. She certainly was neglected! That's what happens to the middle child or cat!

One of the things I like to do is to get into things. I'm always curious about how they would feel. Things like boxes with crinkly paper, my Master's recorder suitcase with the rack to stand up the recorders on and even my Master's camera suitcase. I guess you could call me a curious cat! My folks thought I was pretty silly when I investigated in the dishwasher! After all, I want to learn all about these modern inventions that we have in this house.

And since I'm talking about the kitchen, let me tell you about something else I love to do there. There is a six inch tall railing all along the top of, "oh dear what are those things called?" (Thinking) Oh, yes, they are spindles all around the top of the cupboards. I jump on the counter, then on to the top of the refrigerator (now that's a big word, isn't it?) and on up to the top of the cupboards where I sit down and stick my front paws through those spindles. I've done that as my family thinks it's so funny! There used to be a glass salad bowl up there (I wonder what happened  to it? I haven't seen it for a long time). Anyway, when I was a little kitten I could just fit curled up in that bowl. Richard's wife, Cris, said she would never use that bowl for salad again!

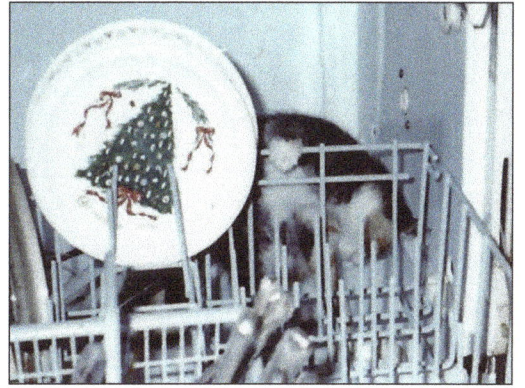

And speaking of people who were not my friends – Mistress's brother, Ted and his wife Rosemary, who lived in Florida would come up to visit sometimes and they hated cats (shame on them!)

But, one time I tried to be friendly and jumped up on Rosemary's lap and she sat quietly and let me do it. And once there was a big surprise. There was a package arrived with two mugs with my picture on it for Master and Mistress's gifts.

There was a group of people who came to our house called the ABC, (Adirondack Baroque Consort), they would practice on their recorders (that's why Master had that suitcase with the wooden racks in it). They would sit in a circle and I would greet them all friendly like and check out their instrument cases also – even sitting in one if I felt like it. Recorders come in all sizes and Mistress was a player of the smallest – the Sopranino. It was very high and shrill and piercing. I wished I could put my paws over my ears! I did let Mistress know what I thought of that "thing" with many loud Meows. It really hurt my ears.

As Pippin said in her autobiography, we each traveled with Master and Mistress in their RVs of which they had three different ones. Pippin went to California but I went to Florida twice and Michigan and Canada also. That's the advantage of having lived twenty one and a half years. I even went to Stowe, Vermont Trapp Family Lodge Guest House when Master and Mistress and Kittie and her three daughters, Bri, Taryn and Caitlyn enjoyed the swimming pool and catching frogs with a net at the Frog Pond. I wished I could have helped them but no animals were allowed on the grounds, so I had to stay in the RV. I did slip out once and led Master a merry chase to get me!

When we went to Florida to visit Ted and Ro (remember they didn't like cats) I had to stay in their screened in back porch. That was okay. There was a little lizard that lived there and I enjoyed watching it.

At home I had my own snug sack. It went along with us too. I liked to go out in our back yard or by the campfire when we were camping in the Adirondacks. Master bought me a red harness and leash and whenever Master or Mistress picked that up I would think to myself, "Oh boy, we're going outside."

I had a couple of games that were a lot of fun. After Master or Mistress went to the grocery store they had those little pieces of paper with how much they spent – I think it was. Master would wrinkle it to a little ball and throw it across the room. I'd run and get it and bring it back to him. Wasn't that pretty smart of me? I think it was!

Another game was quite unique. Mistress lives at Glendale Nursing Home and she is helping to write my autobiography (whew, that was a big word!) Well, back to the game. Master bought a laser (something like a little flashlight). They would shine the light on the wall or even the floor and I would chase it. That was fun!

I like high places also. It is a challenge to get there. Master took a picture of me on top of a ladder. Well, you can see things better high up!

There is another activity I like to do that some people think is amazing but, I just think it's fun. I go into Master and Mistress's bedroom, jump on the bed right on the pretty quilt that Mistress got on her last day of school when she retired. From the bed I jump up to the high dresser (remember the one that Sam, the carrying cat used to swipe socks from?) From the dresser I jump up to the top of the open closet door, walk along it, (see how sure footed I am?) turn around and walk back! Sometimes I sit down and let my feet hang over. Maybe I am amazing – That's really a hard trick to do!

Life was so great living and traveling with Master Bill and Mistress Jane Coffey. It is to be noted that twenty-one and a half years is quite an accomplishment for a cat.

Oh, I forgot to say that I won first prize for my first story, "The One Who Ruled the House." It was for the General Federation of Women's Club in New York State. I'm very proud of that!

So, life went on in the Coffey household. I was getting older and weaker. I was still determined to walk upstairs though I was so weak it took me longer. Daughter, Dr. Barb was there as it was Christmas Eve. She picked me up and we went into the bedroom and we sat down on the bed and I crossed the Rainbow Bridge to Kitty Heaven.

Barb brought me downstairs crying and Master and Mistress saw me and they began to cry too. Mistress and son, Richard, were going to the Christmas Eve service at their church – Burnt Hills United Methodist, that night but they were so sad they couldn't go. See how important I was to them!

SOME ADDITIONAL PICTURES OF CALI!!

Sitting on the camping stool

Hiding in one of Mistress's miniature rooms

How's this for a Christmas Present

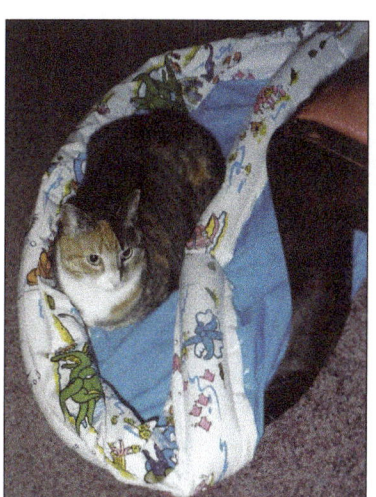
Where is the water for my pool?

Hiding on the shelf of magazines and books

Sitting in Mistress's tote bag

On the windowsill in the den

Hiding under the stool in the Honey RV

Leisure in the RV

AND THEN CAME MAX

My name is Max and I am writing this from Doggie Heaven. I crossed the Rainbow Bridge sometime in the early 1960s. Since the three cats of the Coffey household have written their stories, I thought it only fair that I, the important dog in the family should write my story also.

I do know where I came from. Let me tell you about it. I was born, along with several other puppies (that means very young dogs). See, I have a very good vo-cab-u-lary (whew, that was a big word!) even though I didn't really attend college like one of the Coffey's cats did! (Oh, dear, I'm getting off track. Now where was I? Oh yes, my beginnings!)

My Master, Dick Coffey's (after he was married he wanted to be called Richard or Rich) Mother was a Music Teacher at the nearby grade school and a little first grade boy told her that their dog had just had puppies. So Dick and his Mom went over to this house where six girls and the young boy lived.

I had several brothers and sisters but I licked their hands and rubbed their legs and they picked me! When I got to my new home I was so excited I peed on the bare wood floor and do you know what? It went down through the cracks in the floor to the basement! That was a pretty bad start, wasn't it?

Well, after a while I did learn to go out on the right occasions. There were no leash laws then.

So, I settled down in my lovely new home. But, there was one thing I didn't like! They put me in the basement at night. Now, why did they have to do that? I sat on the landing and whined and cried all night for the first few nights! It served them right.

Since there were no leash laws I could wander the neighborhood and see interesting things. Then I thought it would be fun to bring home some presents for my nice family. I don't remember all of the gifts I brought but I do remember two special ones that I thought my family might like. One was a big brush broom ('course, it didn't have a handle and was awful big for my mouth)! I also brought a little boy's shoe (I thought my Dickie could use one but it was really too small. After that the children in the neighborhood (if they couldn't find their shoes at home) would come to our back door to say, "Did Max bring my shoes here?" No, I only did it that one time and my family weren't very happy about it! Why not? I was only bringing them gifts to show how much I enjoyed living with them!

There was one time when I was so sad I didn't want to eat for a week. Master Bill and Mistress Jane (Dick's Mother and Father) took me to the Veterinarian (that's a big word that means an animal doctor). The Doctor asked, "Has anything unusual happened in your house lately?" Master Bill replied, "Well, our son, Dick, the real owner of this dog, has just gone off to college." The Vet said, "That is the problem. He's missing his Master, I'll give you some pills that will calm his anxiety (see, I'm learning new words all the time!) So I began to take the pills and to eat!

And speaking of college, I'll tell you about a cute incident. Master Dick went to Ithaca College to major in trombone. He still plays it and writes music (that's called composing, you know). My family are all pretty smart. Dick (later, Rich, remember?) has two older sisters, Dr. Barbara Coffey, who is Head of the Child and Adolescent Department at the University of Miami and Kittie, a retired Art Teacher who is still an Artist and also a Creative Writer and takes care of her two little Granddaughters each day.

Mistress Jane had an elderly Aunt Henrietta who lived a couple of miles up a big hill and Dick would be invited up there for a good home cooked meal. Henrietta loved pets and always had a dog and sometimes one or two cats. She had a fault of over feeding her pets. "Oh, just a little snack won't hurt them," was stated several times! So, I knew I would get some doggie food also!

There I go – getting off the subject again! Back to Ithaca! Dick usually didn't live in a dormitory but with other "fellas" in a house on a hill in town. (Most all houses were on hills in Ithaca.) Those were nice places for Dick to walk me – on a leash there, of course.

Well, one day Master and Mistress, Bill and Jane, came to visit their son but he wasn't home. So you know what they did? They called my name through the letter box slot. I recognized their voices and got very excited and stuck my nose out and licked their hands and showed them how much I appreciated (another hard word) their visit.

We did some traveling also but it was before the RV days that the cats talk about in their stories. We traveled in a station wagon (remember that kind of long car? I don't think they make them anymore) with a trailer hooked behind us. That was when cars had front windows with a small window that could be opened. I sure loved to sit up front with Dick and stick my nose out that little window while we were driving and get a nice breeze on my nose.

One time when we were traveling out west, Mistress Jane had a heat stroke and had to lie down on the back seat with cold compresses on her forehead (that was just a wet cloth) so I got to sit up front with my Master and stick my nose out the window.

Let me tell you about the tricks I had to play to get a comfortable seat. We went way up north to Canada and saw and had, many interesting times. I remember once it was so cold I just was shivering and shivering. Master Bill picked me up and put me in the bed between he and Mistress Jane and I was so nice and cozy and could have a good sleep.

I wonder if that was the time that there was such a big thunder storm (Brrrr) that when Master Bill went out of the trailer to unplug the electrics (as they called it in Canada) he stepped into a puddle three inches deep? I was worried he might get electrocuted!

There I go again, I got side tracked. You see, Master Bill thought since we were going to the wilderness of Canada we should take an extra spare tire with us. He put it in the back of the station wagon and I was relegated (fancy word, hey?) to sit in the back with it. Well, I certainly didn't like that arrangement! So this was my trick (or tricks if you want to be specific!) First I put one paw over the back of the back seat (no reaction!) so over goes my other paw. They began to see what was happening and thought it was funny! Then my head was going over – I was getting desperate! Finally I decided to give it my all and jumped all the way over the back of the back seat to sit with my beloved Master Dick! Don't you think that is a good trick? So on to Canada and the city of Banff, which I could look out the window and see the town was full of people, a regular resort town.

On the way there we stopped to see Lake Louise, a beautiful resort lake right in the mountains. I, of course, was on a leash but I wanted to walk in the water. I guess Dick thought dogs weren't allowed in that clear pretty lake so he kept pulling me away and I kept pulling toward the water! We had a regular tug of war and Dick insulted me by calling me a bad dog!

We went to another campground at Jasper National Park. That was an exciting place! Two deer walked into our campsite. I had to bark "Hello" at them but they didn't return my greeting. And, you know what? Mistress went to the evening program and they said a black bear had gone through the program site. I think I'm pretty brave but I sure wouldn't want to get near a bear! I'd be scared to death!!

One thing that happened on that trip was pretty amazing. I hear, though I was left in the trailer, so I didn't know about it until the next day when they talked about it. We were camped about fifteen miles away from a famous mountain carving of four United States Presidents, Mt. Rushmore. The three humans went to see it in the morning, but Master Bill wanted to go back at night to take some night photos. It was a twisting, turning mountainous road and about a mile from the campsite they heard a "clunk". They stopped and found that Master Bill's tripod (a metal thing you put a camera on to steady it to take photos) and Master Bill's sweater had ridden all that way on the roof of the car. Too bad I wasn't with them to warn them that they had left those things on the car roof.

Now we come to the most awful thing that could happen to anyone; be it human or animal! I was in an accident! This is how that terrible thing happened!

Kittie (Dick's next oldest sister) and a friend went for a walk down Charlton Road toward Slim's Market, which was a popular grocery store for that area. They didn't invite me to go along, so I decided to do it anyway. I ran down Charlton Road and when I saw them ran across the road right in front of a car because I was so glad to see them.

Then you know what happened to me? – my left front leg was broken and just hanging there. Kittie and her friend ran back to our house so worried and crying hard. (See how important I was to the Coffey family?) In the meantime I was also running toward home with my leg dragging. Oh how awful it hurt! It hurt so bad I couldn't go any longer, so I just went into somebody's backyard and cried and cried. Those nice people wrapped me up in an old blanket and took me to the Veterinary Hospital. I think they really saved my life and I've been ever so thankful for them.

In the meantime (as they told me later), the Coffey family were looking for me, calling and calling, "Max, M-a-x, M-a-a-x" all down Charlton Road. Finally Mistress Jane suggested they call the Vet's office to see if someone had brought me in. So I had to stay overnight and I was so very happy when they came to get me and took me home.

They thought I would have a long time to re-cup-er-ate (I'm still using hard words you see but I have learned how to sound them out!)

Well, I surprised my people by quickly adapting to my three legged self! I was even able to go up and down the cellar stairs in a couple of days. I'm very strong so I could adapt so well so soon.

So, I became famous as Mrs. Coffey's three legged dog. You know what I used to do? Mistress Jane's music room was very different one year. It was a wooden one room building which had been moved over from being used at the High School after they used it while doing some remodeling there. It had windows on both sides and I used to run up on the snow banks in the winter time and sit and watch Mistress Jane teach her classes. The kids would say, "There's

Mrs. Coffey's three legged dog. If I got too disturbing to the kids in music class, Mrs. Coffey would call our neighbor boy to take me home and close me in our garage. He didn't mind missing music class.

There was a little kind of enclosed covered porch where that building was attached to the main brick building. One day the Principal, Mr. Dunham, came out there to see my Mistress Jane and I barked at him as I was afraid he was going to do something to my Mistress.

I know this is getting "kinda" long but I wanted to write about just a few more incidents that happened while I lived in the Coffey household.

Dick and his sister, Kittie, liked a silly little game I had. I liked to run around the dining room table and nip at the corners of the lace tablecloth hanging down! I don't know why I did that. It was "kinda" fun and gave them all something to laugh about.

I'm not sure of some of the calendar dates that I have in this story. Mistress Jane was looking at past Christmas pictures and found pictures of me on beloved Master Dick's lap on Christmas morning. The second one was dated 1950 and I had only three legs there so I probably had my "bad" accident that year.

When I got to be eight years old, I began to get weaker and weaker and so the Vet decided it was time for me to go to Doggie Heaven. I knew that Dick and all the Coffey family would miss me very much, but I had an exciting and adventurous life being loved by my family and it was time to say "Farewell."

Cute little puppy face!

Max and Pippin

Max, Relaxing in the Living Room

WHAT KIND OF PET SHOULD YOU GET?

Everyone needs a pet
    A soft and furry kitty
To cuddle and to purr for you
    A calico cat is so pretty.

And then there is a dog,
    But there are many a kind.
A Vet could advise you what kind to get.
    And then you can make up your mind.

There are also some unusual ones.
    An iguana or a little pink pig.
But the only trouble with a pig
    They grow so very big.

But there is also a monkey
    That really could be fun!
They could be trained to do tricks for you,
    And keep you on the run.

I must not forget the pony or horse
    A pet they can also be.
Strutting or galloping with you on their back,
    A wonderful sight to see.

I haven't mentioned the goldfish
    Though that's not a kind you can pat.
They look so pretty swimming in their bowl.
    Now what do you think of that?

Some people are allergic to cat fur you know.
    So a ferret can replace that.
It can have a name and play with some toys,
    And take the place of a cat.

So think about these animals you can enjoy.
And which one your family can get.
Because you know, it's universally known –
EVERYONE NEEDS A PET!

ABOUT THE AUTHOR

Jane Coffey is a ninety-nine year old widow with three grown children; a doctor, an artist, and a musician. She lives in a nursing home and is sorry she can't have any pets now — but she keeps herself busy with hobbies including reading, writing poems, playing music, drawing, and coloring.

Jane held a long and melody-filled career as an elementary school music teacher and still plays her piano every day.

www.ingramcontent.com/pod-product-compliance
Lightning Source LLC
LaVergne TN
LVHW072129060526
838201LV00071B/4999